Para Orestes,

Deseándote todas las bendiciones del verdadero amor.

Con todo el cariño de tu profesora,

María Luisa

Febrero, 2007

Housed Under *Glass*

A Story of Desire, Repression, Loss, and Healing

Tras paredes *de cristal*

Una historia de deseo, represión, pérdida y sanación

María Luisa Ortega Hernández

www.cbhbooks.com

Managing Editors: Priscilla Colón, Cliff Clark, and Manuel Alemán
Designer: David Lara

Cover Illustration:
Serenity, oil and gold leaf on wood,
by María del Pilar Ortega Hernández, MD ©2000

Ilustración de la cubierta:
Serenidad, óleo y pan de oro sobre madera,
por María del Pilar Ortega Hernández, MD ©2000

Back cover Photograph / Fotografía de la contracubierta:
José Luis Santana, Tándem Fotógrafos, Madrid, España ©2002

Published in the United States by CBH Books.
CBH Books is a division of Cambridge BrickHouse, Inc.
Cambridge BrickHouse, Inc.
60 Island Street, Lawrence, MA 01840 U.S.A.

Housed Under Glass. A Story of Desire, Repression, Loss, and Healing

Tras paredes de cristal. Una historia de deseo, represión, pérdida y sanación

1. Sexual Abstinence: A Self-Analysis. 2. Female Sexual Dysfunction. 3. Religious Control. 4. Roman Catholic Church. 5. Poetry: Bilingual Edition (English-Spanish).

1. Abstinencia sexual: un autoanálisis. 2. Disfunción sexual femenina. 3. Control religioso. 4. Iglesia Católica. 5. Poesía: edición bilingüe (inglés-español).

Library of Congress Catalog N° 2006004834
ISBN 1-59835-007-2

First Edition

Printed in Canada
10 9 7 8 6 5 4 3 2 1

Housed Under *Glass*

A Story of Desire, Repression, Loss, and Healing

María Luisa Ortega Hernández

Contents

To all women whose petals are fading
in the darkness of a glasshouse,
To those who accompany me with love in the story of my life,
To those who encourage me to follow my childhood dreams
and to deeply satisfy my wildest female yearnings,
To those who will read me one day,
To those who will never be able to read me,

May the Sun shatter the glass that confines them
moved by the blood of my leaves.

Acknowledgements

To the medical team that with such patience, wisdom, and faith took care of my physical, mental, and emotional recovery; especially,

To Susan Kellogg-Spadt, PhD, CRNP, Director of Sexual Medicine, Pelvic and Sexual Health Institute, Graduate Hospital, Philadelphia, Pennsylvania, who diagnosed my case of high tone pelvic floor dysfunction,[1] directed my treatment with other female specialists, and effectively medicated my most intimate area, damaged by twenty years of sexual repression;

To Andrea Branas, MPT, Penn Therapy and Fitness, University of Pennsylvania Medical Center, Philadelphia, Pennsylvania, who took care of my physical therapy through various techniques for the complex rehabilitation of muscles and tissues of the pelvic floor;

To them, and to all who have contributed to the success of my recovery, my deepest gratitude.

[1] To clarify acronyms and some terms, please see the glossary.

My heartfelt thanks to

my beloved sister María del Pilar,

whose essence enriches my life

and adorns the cover of this book.

To the Reader

Dear reader, and female reader even more dear,

You have my wounded soul in your hands. Her few leaves, a condensation of twenty years of sexual repression, scatter themselves in the wind of an open field, the only space able to heal a heart being smothered to death.

Too many years went by before I was diagnosed with a condition that will probably be unknown to you: high tone pelvic floor dysfunction. Vulvar vestibulitis, vaginismus, and dyspareunia are some of the terms that explain the symptoms of an illness that little by little took control of me in the silence of a thousand and one nights of waiting. Although many women suffer from various types of sexual dysfunction, in my case, the causes were solely psychogenic.[2]

Immersed in a repressive religious environment, my obedient spirit controlled a great part of my intellect and my entire will. Premarital sex—which according to the Teaching of the Catholic Church is forbidden by the sixth commandment and punishable by the eternal

[2] In the United States, there is a greater incidence of sexual dysfunction in women (43%) than in men (31%). For more information, see the article written by Edward O. Laumann, PhD, Anthony Paik, MA, and Raymond C. Rosen, PhD, "Sexual Dysfunction in the United States: Prevalence and Predictors," Journal of the American Medical Association 281.6 (Feb. 1999): 537-44.

damnation of the soul—was not part of my repertoire of interaction with the opposite sex, to whom I felt attracted since I was a young girl. While waiting for Prince Charming, total abstinence was required.

When that magical being arrives to rescue the body and soul of a young woman—he willing, as well, to be rescued by her in mutual surrender—the waiting does not create major trauma, as can be verified by my female readers who, in spite of a repressive environment, got married in their early youth. However, although many of us dream of that encounter from our most tender age, sometimes—oh, mystery of life—the waiting prolongs itself indefinitely.

To demand the repression of sexual desire for endless years from a mature human being who loves freely and is freely loved in return carries the gravest of consequences. In fact—I am here to testify to it—it is the abstinence of love in body and soul, and not its practice, that constitutes the true mortal sin. I will explain myself. It is considered a sin that which is willingly committed—in idea, in word, in deed—against the loving plans of God. For example, killing is a sin because a vital, unique, and irreplaceable part of the divine creation is wounded to death. Likewise, mutilation without medical reasons. To cut off a part of the body is an attempt against the very life of a person, a fragmentation of the complete being created by God. Few will disagree. However, many still continue blindfolded, refusing to see that the supreme work of God—the human being, body and spirit—is not dual matter in perpetual conflict, but intimate communion of life and love.

"The Spirit [...] is a carnivorous bird which is incessantly hungry; it eats flesh and, by assimilating it, makes it disappear."[3] This spirit to which Nikos Kazantzakis is referring is the one that the Church has preached to death for so many centuries of its history: it is the spirit that flagellates the body, that subjugates it to shameful food deprivation, that afflicts it with hair shirts, with torments, and with all kinds of sacrifices. To erase the body until the spirit reigns, one of the greatest heresies in history. There is nothing farther from the spirit created by the Most High, breath that enlivens the body in rhythmic harmony. To expect the separation of body and soul is to put two who are one through the slow torture of a sure death.

I am not advocating practicing sex without restrictions either. There are experiences that must be considered with extreme prudence since there is so much at stake. This is one of them. A sexual relationship at thirteen years of age is premature, and, consequently, dangerous. A person at that age is neither physically nor emotionally ready. However, the progressive exploration of one's own sexuality, an integral aspect in the formation of human identity, is necessary long before the awaited nuptial surrender. To deny its existence, to repress it, to suffocate it with taboos buried in the silence of centuries, is to hinder the normal development of a person, whose sexual essence—a divine treasure—is a visible sign of the love of God.

[3] Nikos Kazantzakis, The Last Temptation of Christ, trans. P. A. Bien (New York: Simon and Schuster, 1960) 2.

Parents, priests, teachers, experts, almost all guide with the best intentions. Regretfully, they do not always base themselves on listening, on reflection, on reason. Rules that wound the soul and make the body ill are unacceptable. They are, clearly, empty rules. Who has the right to dictate with whom, how much, when, and how? —Only the person him- or herself, already physically and emotionally mature, protagonist of his, of her story.

I offer my testimony of life, my intimate affliction, and the hope of my recovery with a redemptive purpose. A few days ago, on a cold January morning, while I was awaiting the arrival of the bus, contemplating the dry branches that, naked, were emerging from within the entrails of a landscape covered with snow, a profound revelation made me shudder from the soft center of my being. After an entire life of religious formation, I felt for the first time, in flesh and soul, the mystery of the redemptive value of suffering. I was nailed to that dry and cold tree, alone as so many times, alone as He, shedding my love on a graveyard of agonies.

I knew then that redemption is not for oneself, but for others. But, why did I have to be the one? Why didn't the Sun shatter long before the cold, unmerciful glass that made my spirit captive and my body sick, robbing me of the best twenty years of love? —I don't know, but perhaps there had to be a pain so great that would shout to the four winds a thousand-year-old injustice, embodied in the virginal interlinings of a beautiful girl, all covered in blood.

May my wounded voice, now running free under the April Sun, awaken the sleeping soul, rouse the lifeless body, and come back to me inebriated with new love, with wild passion, with wedding song.

May God want it so.

and you will come to know the truth,

and the truth will set you free.

—John 8:32

A Flower in a House of Glass

Once upon a time, there was a small, sweet, and tender seed, all pure, all white. More than thirty years ago, she was gently planted, while she slept, in a garden made of day. Madonnas, callas, and lilies, violets, tulips, and poppies, hundreds of chosen flowers were growing in fragrance and harmony within the transparent glass of this angelical house. Out of the earth, fertile with love and devotion, emerged a small and delicate stem, beautiful, obedient. Her close friends, dream flowers, reflected the Sun's love with such perfection, that, captivated, the little plant longed to wear one day the same splendid garments, mysterious deference, a heavenly gold bestowed.

On the inner glass of the walls, the morning dew formed a prayer every day: "Oh, Mary, may whoever looks at me, see you!" Faithful guests of the glasshouse, the words took root in her senses, and inhabited, forever, the soft depth of her being. From there, they sang seraphic hymns, rosaries of prayers, litanies, and sermons that would firmly direct the sure course of her first steps. To become a perfect image of purity and obedience would require a strong supplement of grace from a God who, apparently, wanted for the tender woman flower that supernatural goal. They used to tell her that she didn't have to worry. He would be there to console her should she become weak, to encourage her to fulfill His purpose, imposed by Him: to keep herself intact, immaculate, incorrupted, indefinitely.

Trusting, she was growing up under the maternal protection of her artificial land. Specialists in her cultivation used to visit her regularly. They urged her to follow the example of the elders and to avoid, at all cost, the slightest contact with the open field: "We live in the world, but we are not part of it." With the great care of such direction, the tender plant started to blossom. Her beauty was a bliss; such grace, such sweetness to see. Early fruits illuminated the glasshouse with a new hope. She would attend to the withering flowers, encourage those just blooming to keep going. She was learning; she was serving; she was obedient.

A Glasshouse of Love

I was born white,
small, blonde doll.
Green fireflies
whispered to me a song.
Chosen madonna
among thistles and thorns.
In a bubble of love
was nurtured my soul.

The Open Field

A few steps away from the glasshouse, there was the natural world. It was a forbidden place, lacking, seemingly, a plan from above. The seeds would fall where the wind would take them. They would germinate; they would also flourish there. The daisies, neighboring the palm trees; the thistles, softly touching the bellflowers; and the ivies, with mad frenzy, climbing to the naked sky, embracing the love of upright trunks. At first glance, nobody was taking care of the field, open to so much danger. However, an almost magical rhythm was heard in the distance. A tacit order inhabited the Earth, hugging the ground. All beings, unfamiliar with keeping barren rules, pounded with joy under the same Sun of life. How was it possible—the tender flower wondered—that from that profane land, in the midst of so many opposites, one single music emerged, sometimes more joyful than the one sung by her close friends in the house? Through the glass, the flower listened to the charm of the voice running free to the sky, and contemplated, in silence, afar, the horizon of the open field—*ad cautelam*, of course, as she had been told, to avoid the possible contagion with such mortal, unbridled life.

Thoughts

I breathe,
and a soft cry
silent
naked
penetrates the depth of my soul,
remaining there,
curled up in a nest of nostalgias
sleeping in the darkness
of my tender inner recess,
bloody,
deserted without you.

I would like to stay that way,
as the palm tree embracing that lamp post
endlessly caressing his closed eyes
until I could make them open
with his tears in mine
made eternal life
made of love soft light.

Dreams of Spring

Passion burst out of her center with all the strength of an April torrent, and her senses then woke up to the new condition of her being, forever a beating and humid song. At first, her close friends encouraged her with hymns and promises, with legends of other flowers who had found peace in the desert, in service, in obedience. The tender flower meditated then, and sadly drowned of her music, the sound. She had emerged from an extraordinary land, and believed—as she was reminded—that she was called to transform the outside world with the most pure fruits of her exemplary life.

She still did not know it, but her virgin soul had given birth to a son, already eternal: the insatiable desire had been born, the wild longing to surrender, the effusion of a passion that overflowed in sweet humors, and in yearnings of infinite tenderness. Oh, loving flower, my dearest and most intimate female friend, how far you were from knowing that so much growing honey would ferment in a barren sweat, in tears that still come running out of your body of a girl, and that engender, from within your interlinings, flocks of wandering sighs, expiating souls of so many absent kisses.

In the Root of Your Star

In the root of your heart
oh, star of mine!
there are thousands of goblins, charms, and smiles;
your energy, in such sweet beating,
the warmth of your gentle breeze repeating.

Moon of my nocturnal landscape
sun of my conscience and my song
mirror of clamors that cry,
an origin uncertain, a wet pain so far.

Of your first fruit
I wish I could drink
your sempiternal truth
as if from a chalice, asleep.

In you, a tender thorn becoming,
alone, with you, my love,
deep down;
so perfectly nailed
in your body of a man,
that even our souls
I wish
would be pierced
in our cry.

A Walk in the Field

In vain did the flower seek comfort inside the glass of the house. Her yearnings to love did not find an answer from heaven above. Then, the beauty of her early youth looked outside, and a wild flower tapped on her heart, her dreams to let out.

Upon leaving the threshold, she felt the warmth of a new ray of Sun strengthening her, and, looking back, she smiled, pleased to see the divine colors of her flowering body painted on the dew of the glass she was leaving behind.

The tenderness of a first kiss was surrounded by angry thorns, by a coarse voice, of caresses so alone. The gentle flower wanted to love him so truthfully, to heal his wounds, his bitterness to remove, that she let herself be dragged with him by somber castles, empty woods. The curtain of a forbidden world went up one evening full of hopes. A dance of love the tender flower dreaming, where only one long shadow be convening. But the music of the act soon stopped: two separate souls were getting closer; two forms, not one, in the night their hearts transposing. In full bloom, a blinding, a guilty passion thus exposing.

There are hands that hold and uplift, and kisses that resurrect the soul that has gone afar. But the magic of love only works before other hands opening up in turn, and in other mouths that pronounce that spell of honey that reaches the soul and runs through the body in a spasm of joy, of members that throw themselves to the encounter of that which is theirs, and that claim it in an eternal embrace. And since then one's breath belongs to the other one already, to that dear inhabitant of our most intimate humidity, where to the rhythm of the two stars are born that do not fall in the night and tenderness that melts in soft, tiny drops of heavenly sky.

A Love to Remember

"... *forgetting is so long*." His love caressed my eighteen years with the softness of a teddy bear, still seating on my pillow. What can I say of that love! A smile in the air, a kiss, a dream bursting in the soul with the sweetness of the eyes of a girl who wants to be a woman, and cannot. A free, playful flower was intensely enjoying the moment; his soul, so unaware of the torment beginning to stir inside his dear Marisita. Together, they played with love for a while—so brief—and the trail of his departure buried caresses that still agonize in the far embrace of a memory in bloom.

In Your Oasis

From the sweet oasis of your body
my soul yearns to get drunk one day.
My body in a passionate kiss
all your soul breathing,
the tender fruit of my poetry releasing.

To sink in the thickness of your pine trees,
silver hearts of the sea,
to drink the eucalyptus of your land
and in the frost of your breath, shipwrecked be found.

To shatter the mirror of this waiting
to fall in the center of your peace
to run in your valley without thorns
to sing my truth in your star, all me.

Without glass feeling.
My body living.
Yours my fragrance, my soul,
          and flower never more.

Shadows

The visit of a dark blackbird tore the tender wound of absence, and in a hollow of thistles and dry bones her heart of pollen remained, hurt and alone, in the agony breathing the dead dust that a sad flight of lies lifted.

A new ray of Sun slowly renovated the torn tissue of desire. A beautiful tree he was, fresh shade and pleasing to the eye. In the field of his branches the tender flower girl worked, and, without she willing, her soul, his green leaves were seeking. Each day, the idea of his charms she caressed, the flattery of his tongue captivated her; all disguises of a love hiding from her, foreign language to a bright flower, in pure dreams giving herself. Five springs full of hopes, beating with love, in faithful waiting, poured out on the sand of his hands, of his body of a man, of his lips longing for another love, from her so far.

Delirium

Hole of soft sorrows,
my heart dyed in blood your somber offering.

Butterfly of celestial cartilage
gray sky
dry rain
tainted spell.

From the abyss, you invite me,
ivy dreamed of diamonds,
to bathe in the silence of your frost
to drink your ashes over a low flame.

The earth moans
the world forgets
the waters tremble,
in pain,
and you,
night of mine,
erupt your rubies from the soft depth
of my treasure,
all covered in blood.

In the gloomy moon of disenchantment
the barren land of your love was burning.
And a tender, blooming voice
shattered the ice over the wounded glass
with new agonies from afar…

I am the drop of a tear
I am a tear that sings
I am a note; I am a song
I am a soul that bleeds
drop by drop
all me.

Mirage

I am a tiny drop of crystallized dew
that you elevated to the status of a star.

My hands
trembling at dawn
passionately
pounding
for your night.

My agonizing body
wearing a mirage
to the rhythm of a foreign music
            your ethereal dance
                        fleshless foam
                        empty of the blood of the wild.

Oh, enchanted king,
seed of tears and sand,
why did you make me a star
if out of your beautiful lamp
needles of fast-flowing silver
as in a hard dam of salt
jumped out in nebular whips
and made my quest rest
in tiny pieces of glass!

Sighs

Dreams
vain illusions
in white shrouds
accompany me tonight
weeping at the edge of a cold tomb.

In the darkness, they besiege my image
desolate and sad
losing her petals,
alone,
in the forgotten corner
of a distant glasshouse.

My life basted with caresses
your pattern.
So many times your hands
so many your lips
on the warm cloth
weaved by my longing.

Sad, painful drops
jumped out of my soul tonight
drank by insensible tentacles
dry
stepped on without mercy
forgotten
in the green darkness of this rug,
awful company
to an infinite exile.

One More Night

Seven years after our goodbye as children, you passed by my life once again. I remembered then our blossoming love, and of your young bud, its mad yearnings, seeds that fertilized my soul with children that still look for you, smothered to death, one by one, in a painful torrent of blood and of wounded hopes between my white sheets. That is how you found me, love only absent in body, with the gagged passion of a fierce desire, forbidden from my womanly paradise by deaf voices that, in the midst of litanies and alleluias, lifted up their disconcerting song to the Sun, a life sentence, the most cruel death of all: my flowering body, such divine treasure, shivering with love behind an impenetrable display window, a glass so cold.

And one night, we went out holding hands. In the noisy room, we shared our most precious dreams. I showed you my soul then—always fond, forever open to you. I told you of my aching yearnings, of my continued desire to surrender a full flower, of my long waiting, deeply misunderstood, by many rejected. And your body, captivated by a different scent, with a kiss on my forehead left; my blooming fragrance, kept at such high price, you, as others, declined.

I do not blame you now for not wanting a love made only of dreams until in nuptial commitment I gave myself to you—contrary to what you thought, a day not so distant from you. I do blame you, though, for shutting your soul before the anguish that desolated mine; for not loving me enough as to dare to rescue me with the weight of your body of a man, in your surrender purifying the dark poison that had long ago tainted my blood.

Your Marisita was already ill, and she had no suspicion. Of her first trip to the open field, she returned with such sorrow, a melancholy so deep, that in the glasshouse once more protection she sought; blooming resolutions to be better she hoped. Her soul, new guides tending; greater penances directing. Her sad spirit, accepting; her body, every part, inside converting; all traces of an evil, from within assailing. Ten more years would go by until a diagnosis was pronounced, a mysterious condition her flowering body contracted, frozen by an eternal dew of pleas, of supplications unfulfilled.

Absence of You

To feel you absent is what pierces my soul the most
to know you are gone
sailing inside other living eyes
as mine die in sad torrents of lies,
in mute memories never alive.

Drops of myself shed
empty me out of a yesterday that was not mine.

Your eyes inside my soul
visit me during long hours
and they contemplate in each corner
broken images
dreams not dreamt
          and my open hands.

Wounded Hopes

In the distance, your voice, already mature, tried to apologize for an absence not announced. You said that you loved me too much then and that because of that you left. For long hours, your words resounded in my soul. Impossible to understand your goodbye never expressed. When one truly loves, one's soul gets near, sharing sorrows and hopes, listening to the cry of a tear; caressing trembling hands, kissing tired lips with devotion, accompanying the steps of a body that was loved, and that, in silence, continues to be loved, still.

You wanted then to live the moment, dearest name of my heart, without ties, without sorrows, free from your blooming flower, whose soul was bleeding in pain, whose bright body she reserved. Three years later, you were getting married to a body in whose soul you did not dwell. You loved me and because of that you left? True love never dies—my soul whispered a bit late. It loves in the distance that which the body, indisposed, can't. Your love could have healed me—I do know—and you did not love me then, as you do not love me now.

Memories

Like two young girls in love,
the pupils of my eyes look inside you
and my yearnings escape, madly, from my mouth.

Oh, memory, living in my mind
never presence of flesh becoming.
Poetic corpus, I dream of you
and in my bed only idea, chimera,
and fog.

I live kissing you
in my nights of memories unborn
but memories made nonetheless
not with the experience of a life
but with the life of an idea
that leaves rushing from its cell
travels through forbidden paradises
and returns pregnant with desires,
virginal passions that
in burning madness
wake me up to a feverish world
and help me
not to die while living.

I am a flower perishing in the cold.
Frosts of abandonment freezing my bones
roots drowning in lies
and my petals,
pale thoughts,
overflowing naked
on each infinite night.

Because so many eyes that once saw me
left in me the dreadful mark
of a goodbye—no, thank you—
that, when the Sun sets,
becomes the same oasis of illusions
over the echo of your voice, dormant and far.

Scent of a Woman

Day and night I walk by streets and paths, alleys sleeping in the mysterious depth of an idea. You have lived in me for so long, that the mere memory of your image enlivens the dream of an almost blind hope. For many years now, I have been searching for you in the whispering of a voice trapped in time. When I wake up under the warmth of the full moon of smiles covering my lightness—so many times—a sigh, empty of your pattern, emits the sweetest thought of all: being with you.

I look for you from within my wounded core, weeping drops of honey that get lost far from your mouth. When will you caress my stem and calm my burning leaves, my petals, my pollen, when? When will your bud, my love, baptize my deep, white roots? A wild flower is what I want to be now, running free under the Sun through prairies with no bounds, quickly pulling off scales that lean out of the door of this piece of glass buried in the depth of my waiting, and, already all of me, rest naked in your arms, a woman forever yours, body and soul intoxicating, humid fragrance of the wild.

Dissonance

A majestic tree visited one day the dark house of glass. The tune of his voice attracted the passion of her tender soul in heat. Resting under his shade, her prayers seemed repaid, and both together started a soft song to raise. A just man she wanted beside; in the scrubland, she would have found him at hand. They walked a short while on the path of the Lord, and the sky, open with dreams, with fears became filled. The music into a coarse tone changed; caresses, fierce jealousy became; sudden laziness, he revealed; obedience and submission, all demanding from the girl. Unknown worlds will never get along; the honey of sweet flowers was not made for the pleasure of crude taste.

Escape

I would empty myself of me tonight
if it were possible
exiling from my soul so much black sorrow.
Dreams, fantasies, chimeras,
to have once loved a love wishing.

If out of myself I could leave,
I would fly out of my body a great distance;
already idea and not a person,
in me neither flower nor sweetness existing.

Because in the inner core of my soul
wounded memories lie
deep sores of shattered dreams
sleeping ghosts that silently lean out of me
living witnesses of a never-ending pain.

Your Edge, My Sorrow

A husband is he who rests his head
on the lap of his faithful beloved.
Sobbing, tears, fierce caressing,
ivory and silver, pale gold,
honey of love that melts in a kiss
in the humid ivy
to the final pore.

Light piercing my deepest space
with the magical smile of his pure eyes,
you nailed in my soul forever
the warm passion of his scent of a man.

In the root of his star I dreamt one day,
and the cry of a girl became frost and sand.

Lament

Soft petals wounded by the bitterness of an absence
shiver, alone, before a day that never comes.

My small sanctuary all deserted
of eyes
of hands
of kisses
sighs for an eternal watering of blood
of long roots
of words made of honey
pouring a thousand I-love-you's
into the forgotten well of so many thirsty lips.

A hidden pollen that sleeps in eternal depths
maturing ideas
engenders children who fly away as butterflies,
goblins that inhabit falling stars
and abandon,
without her soul,
the weak fragrance of a honeysuckle.

The wind caresses me
every night with his manly song,
and my tissues,
tied up,
cry from afar.

Desert Storm

You flew over my field one day later, herb of mint apparently good. Your willowy body, the softness of your skin, the sweetness of your kisses made me dream of an enchanted world, populated by nymphs of gold. Holding your arm, my steps seemed secure; your details, many; your music of love, plenty. Little angels were washing the city, and you were captivated—so I believed—by the thousand crazy ideas of a girl. One evening of passion, you leaned into the clear waters of my soul. A quick look you did not stand, and, frightened, you left me behind; too perfect for yours, your last sentence, goodbye. In less than nine hours, the mint of your voice gave birth to infinite worms that pierced my wounded core, a nest full of blood, then housing new children of fraud.

Calvary

If calvary were one
dying would not be a continuous agony.
One would die once, and period.
But black heralds persecute us from up close
and every day gives birth to tomorrows of infinite crosses
of dark nights
of endless cries.

And we dream of the day of glory.
We think: my calvary is over.
Now it is my turn to live a little
to harvest smiles and carnations
to drink looks and to wear new hugs.

Oh, mirage, the dream that wishes to live life to the fullest!
Our days are bitter drops drowning
feet that walk alone
that alone travel in search of others
that are never found
that have left
or that have not yet arrived.

Stars

There are few, but certain moments will forever shine over the immortal firmament of desire: a first look, the soft pressure of an embracing body, the unexpected humidity of a kiss that inexplicably says goodbye, and the magic of that call just about halfway through life.

Resurrection

My soul evokes your body in the midst of silence
upon hearing you in the time of an already absent space.

To remember your voice that autumn Friday
to listen from your lips the mention of my name
to feel a gust of violence so soft
in my spirit your voice
your breath made word
my name in your lips invoking sentiment
a baptism anew
a sacrament of love.

Your word takes me to a time long gone
where my desire to love you has remained trapped
wrapped in a shroud of withered kisses
of lullabies that cry
in silence
the dream of a slow smothering to death.

A goodbye that does not want to be said
resurrects the ghost of a song already mute.
Outside of me I observe her face
her smile of a girl
her infinite tenderness
her soul that sleeps awaiting a body
her body that suffers in merciless anguish.

Wounded and naked
my self
all yours
weeps again saying another goodbye to you.

Sweet heart of mine,
may you enjoy so much love with her
as your blooming girl
once again
offered you.

Blue

My newborn caresses
jumped
naked
into a green world
crazy to quench your yearnings
one
by
one
and mine drown in your peace,
beloved bud of my soul.

But my beautiful hands are already blue
and blue drops daily fade a pale face
that dreamt one dawn of smiles and emeralds
and bled to death her yearnings dreaming,
alone,
in the distance.

And it is that blue wings grew on your body
taking you afar
and the silence you left behind is already a blue sky
that steams the soul.
Your green depth
your long hands
your pure essence
rejecting my humidity in full bloom
today as yesterday

for another fragrance far less sweet
for other eyes yet not so bright
and for a body, my love,
that will never learn to dance
to the warm rhythm
of the soul once yours and mine.

And that light that used to illuminate of my core
the most hidden word
is heartrending penumbra, all blue frost by now.
My field, green one day,
my mount, ambrosia in song,
blue memories of a wounded life,
the saddest graveyard of them all.

Thanks

Majestic trees, strong trunks, various species of the sea approached the flower, and one by one her sanctity admired. So many went by her life, sighing for her love, so many who wanted her body, her soul, and her honor above. To them all the flower thanks for crossing her path, teaching her lessons of love, of truth, and of life. She also apologizes for not being able to give them that which of her they sought without lies, without evil proceedings.

A Look Behind

For many years now, the flower has been meditating deeply. She remembers so much lost passion, so much music sleeping. She reflects now on her past behavior; so many empty norms, so many nights, so cold. The soul, it is true, must first be exposed; little by little—she has been told—to avoid a mortal fall. Without her breath, it is impossible the rest, which is the body that surrenders in a dance of nuptial steps. Love in body and soul is true wedding of all, of two souls and two bodies who one already become.

Now the flower wishes to go back in time, and in full body to love with her soul from above. A mission for her already impossible to achieve, as that of those who in separating body and soul insist. A ray of Love merged flesh and spirit into one single self. Not to kiss with one's soul is to kiss with deceit.

Rock Bottom

A not far encounter hurt her so deeply, that the screaming of her body made her being shudder. It was a withered tree—now she clearly sees—an empty ghost, a bitter grave from below. The flower, still tender, wanted her love to apply to so many ugly wounds and his so many torments to cure. Along with her pure soul, her body of a girl to surrender, behind the eternal glass of a thousand one nights in sweetness protected.

The nausea of the past returned, with the same intensity now, result of that poison that wanted her passion pulled up. He tried to be patient, to help her with tenderness, but the flower was not able to bend her tense petals, her leaves to surrender. The patience of his hands temerity became, and his voice, that used to charm her, total fear and distress. The frightened girl ran away from such a hostile land, her dreams stepped on while awake, her dearest April romance.

A Look Within

Promptly, she left in search of a clear explanation. Several doctors saw her before a diagnosis was offered. An internal dysfunction presented; a long treatment awaited. She learned all she could about this condition, that many times traumas are the precise reason. The flower analyzed each detail of her life, each encounter, each thorn, and, of all, each friendly voice. She observed her beliefs, her guidelines, her struggles subsisting; her moments of joy, her rejections, her wounds all existing.

Soon she remembered a physical discomfort. Every passionate kiss her body uplifted was followed by trembling and fear coexisting. When the kiss became a nuptial foredance, nausea from within was just the normal thing. Bathed in her sweet moisture, an intimate pain compressed her in distress. There was nobody to whom this to express. Distance and prayer her guides prescribed to avoid the sin by the body prepared in such act. The girl endured in tears painful, fierce lashes unkind. Muscles prepared to open up in surrender, with a command to retreat, their thousand veins suddenly refrained. Nausea became more severe then; the pain, so much deeper, in her most sealed recess.

Cruel Spell

In the secrecy of the glasshouse, a mortal virus was growing under the shadow of a cassock eaten away by time. When the tiny seed, asleep, for the first time opened her pure eyes to the sky, a dark gauze clouded the brightness of the Sun that in all splendor penetrated deep within the glass so cold. Inside the vigilant walls, choirs of deaf voices were repeating, for centuries old now, the same universal song: "The flesh had to be kept intact, immaculate, incorrupted, indefinitely; kill its desires, one by one, or else damnation would befall." The merciless tune worked its mortal charm on the girl. A terror to sin already dominated within: her mind, her transparent spirit, and, of her most sensual flesh, each passionate space.

Wound

Oh, dagger,
cutting
one
by
one
my transparent edges;
deep slice
severing my first yearning;
blasphemy of a Sun
that warming us He hated.

Dreams, kisses, caresses,
a feast from afar.

Frozen sighs
long processions of prayers
walking barefoot
                    inside
steaming with the blood of a girl
the betraying blade
of a merciless glass buried
                    deep within
my soul
my body,
a sacrosanct space,
                    in secrecy becoming
                    a dark, an eternal sacrilege.

The Price of Virtue

An obedient flower wanted in heaven to dwell. She thought that her guides were going to take care of her. That she should patiently await her beloved to arrive; that virtue would make her stronger, of her a monument sculpting, a living example to other flowers becoming. The sweet flower reached perfection so high, that she stayed, my little one, inside her artificial house, all alone behind the glass. So many eyes admired her beauty, so many desired her figure, but not one dared to take her; to think of it was almost a profanation; to her own unhappiness, an icon of sanctity she remained for veneration.

Twenty years of shivering and nausea, ten of the memory of the first painful contraction, a body and a soul wounded by deaf voices, a flower losing her petals alone, a music drowning inside, drops poured out in the wind, I.

Bound

There were no physical causes, but painful dysfunction such evil became. Through the spirit it entered the mind, and, from there, the orders went to every corner in sight. To the one who may still not believe, let her, let him try to forbid from the body the same passion over twenty years of merciless contractions. A deep discomfort of spirit will travel to the stomach for a while; so much revulsion and nausea in fear of not acting right. If she finds herself in the arms of a mutual love, and the voices of the spirit soften their deaf cry, the mind will double up efforts not to lose the place behind; invisible messengers will command, armed with laces and ties for the muscles to bind. The body, however, will continue its sexual dance; for that it was made by such immortal design. When the restriction prolongs itself for years on end, and, instead of sweetness, the muscles ties only learn, the day of sorrow will arrive—that day in September, so sad—when there will be no caress that will be able to break the coral that bonds a hidden heavenly cave.

Unbind him, and let him go free.

—John 11:44

Darkness

The recovery process has been complex and slow; the therapy, intense; more than infinite the loss. Veins dilated in springs of blood, muscles and tissues compressed, already impassable, punctured by long nerves, their roots in the air, burning needles piercing my self before the soft touch dreamt for years on end.

My blooming pain demanded then a potent medicinal balm, and from the Sun the love of His providential warmth. —They would not be, for now, those long hands of which the girl used to dream that would save her one night; her beautiful blonde hands rescuing his hands in an intimate dance.

There were days eternal of agony and horror. Under a perpetual storm the flower seemed to dwell, and the full eye of the storm she would feel break over her. The bright sky, in serene, kind distance, afar. When the flower saw that the storm was building up from her holiest depth, sweeping away each pore, each vessel, and each space, and that her field, green one day, was now a blue cry, so dense, the eye of the storm entire, hurting her in mortal care, my little one had to pick up her abused petals by herself, her rejected pollen, her fresh, unwanted scent, and courageously save her body and her spirit, one single passion, one single love on the cross nailed.

A Dance in Spring

Today, the flower runs free through the open field. Her bright body, silenced for so long, purifies itself, naked, in the scream that passionately flows from her wounded core, a torrent pouring itself into the depths of a land full of blood, inhabited by long roots, endlessly white and gold.

Under the radiant April Sun, the beautiful girl in bloom dresses up in green, dreaming, once again, of that idyllic dance caressing the upcoming night with the magical swinging of one long single shadow in love.

Breathing the sacred warmth of the Sun,
falling asleep amidst the thickness of your white hands
–eucalyptus and silver entangled in blonde threshing floors–
my humid fragrance of the wild playing with you,
with my hands of a girl, with your body of a man,
with a love forevermore.

He who has ears to hear,

let him hear.

—Luke 8:8

Glossary

CRNP. Certified Registered Nurse Practitioner. In the United States, a nurse specialized in the physical and psychosocial diagnosis of patients, as well as in their treatment. Due to expert training, she or he can prescribe medications and carry out a variety of medical procedures.

dyspareunia. Painful coitus or painful attempted coitus. Deep genital or pelvic pain experienced by a woman before, during, or after intercourse. It can be caused by local trauma (among others: congenital malformation, infection, inflammation of the vestibular glands, estrogenic deficiency, tumors) or by psychological factors (vaginismus).

EdD. *Educationis Doctor*. Doctor of Education.

heresy. (figure of speech) Great damage or torment unjustly inflicted on a person.

LPC. Licensed Professional Counselor.

MA. *Magister Artium* (m.), *Magistra Artium* (f.). Master of Arts.

MD. *Medicinae Doctor.* Doctor of Medicine.

MPT. Master of Physical Therapy.

NCC. National Certified Counselor.

pelvic floor. Muscles, ligaments, and tissues located at the base of the abdomen, whose hammock-like structure holds the uterus, the bladder, the urethra, and the rectum. The pelvic floor muscles are also known as "love muscles" since they play a primary role in women. They are used during sexual intercourse, pregnancy, and childbirth, as well as in urinating and emptying the bowels. They react to coughing, laughing, sneezing, and contractions of the abdomen. When these muscles become weak, part of the physical therapy focuses on Kegel exercises, owing their name to Arnold H. Kegel, twentieth-century US gynecologist and obstetrician.

PhD. *Philosophiae Doctor.* Doctor of Philosophy.

psychogenic. (adjective) Originating in the mind or in an emotional or mental conflict.

sexual dysfunction. Disorder in the normal function of sexuality upon the quantitative or qualitative imbalance of one of its components: the mind (thoughts and emotions) or the body (nervous, circulatory, muscular, and endocrine systems). Physical factors usually carry psychological problems, and psychological factors, in turn, create or aggravate physical problems.

vaginismus. A sudden and painful involuntary conditioned contraction of the muscles surrounding the vagina. It is caused by the conscious or unconscious desire of the woman to avoid penetration. Among the physical factors responsible for this condition are lesions, ulcers, and the inflammation of the vagina. Among the psychological causes, the most frequent are sexual traumas: rape, incest, fear or aversion to coitus, a repressive family environment, and a religious practice centered on the control of a body perceived as enemy of the spirit and an obstacle to eternal salvation.

vulvar vestibulitis. Inflammation of the vulvar vestibule. It is one of several vulvar pain syndromes causing dyspareunia. See **vulvodynia**.

vulvodynia. Literally, "painful vulva." The term refers to several painful conditions affecting the female genitalia. The most common is vulvar vestibulitis syndrome (VVS), characterized by the inflammation of the vestibular glands: Bartholin glands (after the Danish anatomist Caspar Bartholin Secundus, 1655-1738) and Skene glands (after the famous Scottish gynecologist who migrated to the U.S., Alexander Johnson Chalmers Skene, 1837-1900). Although the cause still remains unknown, several factors may contribute to its onset: infections, irritations, and neuromuscular injuries. As a result, the vestibule becomes inflamed and the glands hypersensitive (both staying that way unless treated), which makes any contact—whether neutral (tampons), or stimulating (sexual penetration)—the source of intolerable physical burning and pain. For more details, see the informative brochure by Susan Kellogg-Spadt, PhD, Managing Vulvar Vestibulitis and Sexual Pain: A Guide for Women and Their Partners, 2001; and the article "Vulvar Vestibulitis and Sexual Pain: New Insights," published by Susan Kellogg-Spadt, PhD, and Jennifer L. Giordano, EdD, in the journal The Female Patient, Vol. 27, April, 2002.

Tras paredes *de cristal*

Una historia de deseo, represión, pérdida y sanación

María Luisa Ortega Hernández

Índice

A todas las mujeres cuyos pétalos palidecen
en un oscuro invernadero,
A las que me acompañan con amor en la historia de mi vida,
A las que me animan a que siga la ilusión de mis juegos de niña
y a que colme hasta el fondo mis ansias salvajes de hembra,
A las que me lean algún día,
A las que nunca podrán leerme,

Que el Sol rompa el cristal que las encierra
conmovido por la sangre de mis hojas.

Agradecimientos

Al equipo médico que con tanta paciencia, sabiduría y fe se encargó de mi recuperación física, mental y emocional; en especial,

A Susan Kellogg-Spadt, PhD, CRNP, Directora de Medicina Sexual, Instituto de Salud Pélvica y Sexual, Graduate Hospital, Filadelfia, Pensilvania, quien me diagnosticó un caso extremo de disfunción del fondo pélvico[1], dirigió mi tratamiento con otras especialistas, y medicó eficazmente mi área más íntima, dañada por veinte años de represión sexual;

A Andrea Branas, MPT, Penn Therapy and Fitness, Centro Médico de la Universidad de Pensilvania, Filadelfia, Pensilvania, quien se encargó de mi fisioterapia mediante diversas técnicas para la compleja rehabilitación de músculos y tejidos del fondo pélvico;

A ellas, y a todos los que han contribuido al éxito de mi recuperación, mi más profundo agradecimiento.

[1] Para la aclaración de siglas y de algunos términos, véase el glosario.

Mi gratitud a

mi amada hermana María del Pilar,

cuya esencia enriquece mi vida

y adorna la cubierta de este libro.

Al lector

Querido lector, y lectora aun más querida:

Tienes en tus manos mi alma herida. Sus breves hojas, condensación de veinte años de represión sexual, se lanzan al viento de un campo libre, único espacio capaz de sanar un corazón que muere de asfixia.

Pasaron demasiados años hasta que me diagnosticaron una afección que será para ti probablemente desconocida: un caso extremo de disfunción del fondo pélvico. Vestibulitis vulvar, vaginismo y dispareunia son algunos de los términos que explican los síntomas de un mal que poco a poco tomó posesión de mí en el silencio de mil y una noches de espera. Aunque muchas mujeres padecen de diferentes tipos de disfunción sexual, en mi caso, las causas fueron únicamente psicógenas[2].

Inmerso en un ambiente religioso represivo, mi espíritu obediente controlaba gran parte de mi intelecto y mi entera voluntad. El acto sexual prematrimonial —prohibido por el sexto mandamiento y penalizado con la condenación eterna del alma, según el Magisterio de la

[2] En los Estados Unidos, existe una mayor incidencia de disfunción sexual en la mujer (43%) que en el hombre (31%). Para más información, véase el artículo escrito por Edward O. Laumann, PhD, Anthony Paik, MA, y Raymond C. Rosen, PhD, "Sexual Dysfunction in the United States: Prevalence and Predictors" ["La disfunción sexual en los Estados Unidos: prevalencia y factores de riesgo"], Journal of the American Medical Association 281.6 (Feb. 1999): 537-44.

Iglesia Católica— no tenía cabida en mi repertorio de comunicación con el sexo opuesto, al que me sentí atraída desde niña. Mientras se aguardaba al Príncipe Azul, abstinencia total.

Cuando llega ese ser mágico a rescatar el cuerpo y el alma de una joven —dispuesto él, a su vez, a ser rescatado por ella en una entrega mutua—, la espera no causa mayores traumas, como podrán verificar mis lectoras que, a pesar de una atmósfera represiva, se casaron en su primera juventud. No obstante, aunque muchas soñamos con ese encuentro desde la más tierna edad, a veces —oh, misterio de la vida— la espera se prolonga indefinidamente.

Exigir del ser humano maduro que ama libremente y es libremente correspondido la represión del deseo sexual durante años sin límite conlleva consecuencias gravísimas. De hecho —estoy yo para testificarlo—, es la abstinencia del amor en cuerpo y alma, y no su práctica, lo que constituye el verdadero pecado mortal. Me explico. Se considera pecado lo que voluntariamente se realiza —en idea, en palabra, en acto— contra los designios del amor de Dios. Por ejemplo, matar es pecado porque se hiere hasta la agonía mortal a una parte vital, irrepetible e irremplazable de la creación divina. De la misma manera, la mutilación sin razones médicas. Cortar del cuerpo una parte es un atentado contra la propia vida de la persona, una fragmentación del ser completo que Dios creó. Pocos estarán en desacuerdo. Sin embargo, cuántos siguen con las vendas puestas, negados a ver que la obra suprema de Dios —el ser humano, cuerpo y espíritu— no es materia dual en perpetuo conflicto de contrarios, sino íntima comunión de vida y amor.

"El Espíritu [...] es un pájaro carnívoro que está incesantemente hambriento; come carne y, al asimilarla, la hace desaparecer"[3]. Este espíritu al que se refiere Nikos Kazantzakis es aquél que la Iglesia ha predicado hasta la enfermedad durante tantos siglos de su historia: es el espíritu que flagela al cuerpo, que lo somete a penosas privaciones de alimentos, que lo atormenta con cilicios, con sacrificios y con todo tipo de martirios. Anular el cuerpo hasta que el espíritu reine, una de las mayores herejías de la historia. No hay nada más ajeno al espíritu creado por el Altísimo, hálito que anima al cuerpo en rítmica armonía. Pretender separar cuerpo y alma es propiciar a dos que son uno la lenta tortura de una muerte segura.

No abogo tampoco por una práctica sexual sin restricciones. Hay experiencias que deben medirse con suma prudencia puesto que es mucho lo que se arriesga. Ésta es una de ellas. Una relación sexual a los trece años es prematura y, por ende, peligrosa. La persona no está entonces preparada ni física ni emocionalmente. Sin embargo, la exploración progresiva de la propia sexualidad, aspecto integral en la formación de la identidad humana, es necesaria mucho antes de llegar a la ansiada entrega nupcial. Negar su existencia, reprimirla, sofocarla mediante tabúes enterrados en el

[3] Mi traducción: Nikos Kazantzakis, The Last Temptation of Christ [La última tentación de Cristo], trad. P. A. Bien (Nueva York: Simon and Schuster, 1960) 2.

silencio de los siglos, atrofia el desarrollo normal del ser, cuya esencia sexual —tesoro divino— es claro reflejo del amor de Dios.

Los padres, los sacerdotes, los maestros, los expertos, casi todos guían con las mejores intenciones. Lamentablemente, no siempre se basan en la escucha, en la reflexión, en la razón. Ante leyes que hieren el alma y enferman el cuerpo, no hay autoridad que valga. Son, a todas luces, leyes vanas. ¿Quién tiene el derecho a dictar con quién, cuánto, cómo y cuándo? —Únicamente el propio ser, ya maduro física y emocionalmente, protagonista de su historia.

Ofrezco mi testimonio de vida, mi íntima aflicción y la esperanza de mi recuperación con un propósito redentor. Hace pocos días, en una mañana fría de enero, mientras esperaba la llegada del autobús y contemplaba las ramas secas que se alzaban, desnudas, desde las entrañas de un paisaje cubierto de nieve, una revelación profunda me estremeció desde el blando fondo de mi ser. Después de una vida entera de formación religiosa, sentí por primera vez, en carne y alma, el misterio del valor redentor del sufrimiento. Estaba yo clavada en ese árbol seco y frío, sola como tantas veces, sola como Él, derramando mi amor en un camposanto de agonías.

Entonces supe que la redención no es propia, sino ajena. Pero, ¿por qué yo? ¿Por qué el Sol no rompió antes el frío cristal que, inmisericorde, cautivó mi espíritu y enfermó mi cuerpo, robándome mis mejores veinte años de amor? —No lo sé, pero quizá tenía que haber un dolor tan grande que gritara a los cuatro vientos una injusticia milenaria, encarnada en las virginales entretelas de una bella niña ensangrentada.

Que mi voz herida, que ya corre libre bajo el Sol de abril, recuerde al alma dormida, despierte al cuerpo inerte y regrese a mí embriagada de amor nuevo, de pasión salvaje, de boda plena.

Ojalá.

y conoceréis la verdad,

y la verdad os hará libres.

—Juan 8:32

Una flor de invernadero

Érase una vez una semillita tierna, dulce, toda ella blanca. Hace más de treinta años que manos solícitas la plantaron, dormida, en un jardín de cristal. Lirios, calas y azucenas, violetas, tulipanes y amapolas, cientos de flores escogidas crecían en fragancia y armonía en ese invernadero angelical. De la tierra fecundada de cariño y devoción, brotó un tallito delicado, precioso, obediente. Sus compañeras, flores de ensueño, reflejaban el amor del Sol con tal perfección, que la plantita, extasiada, ansiaba lucir algún día aquellas galas, deferencia misteriosa, divina dádiva.

Sobre el vidrio interior de las paredes, el rocío de la mañana formaba a diario una plegaria: "¡Oh, María, que quien me mire te vea!" Fieles huéspedes del invernadero, las palabras fecundaron sus sentidos y poblaron, para siempre, el suave fondo de su ser. Desde allí entonaban cánticos seráficos, rosarios de oraciones, letanías y sermones que encaminarían con firmeza la derrota segura de sus primeros pasos. Llegar a ser imagen perfecta de pureza y obediencia exigiría un fuerte suplemento de gracia de parte de un Dios que, al parecer, quería para la florecita mujer esa meta sobrenatural. Que no se preocupara, le decían. Allí estaría Él para consolarla cuando desfalleciera, para animarla a cumplir Su propósito por Él impuesto: mantenerse intacta, inmaculada, incorrupta, indefinidamente.

Crecía, confiada, bajo el amparo maternal de su jardín artificial. Especialistas en su cultivo la visitaban asiduamente. La exhortaban a seguir el ejemplo de los mayores y a evitar, a toda costa, el más ligero contacto con el campo exterior: "Vivimos en el mundo, pero no somos de él". Con el esmero de tal dirección, la plantita comenzó a florecer. Daba gloria contemplar su hermosura; tantas gracias a la vista, tantas dulzuras. Precoces frutos iluminaron el invernadero con una nueva esperanza. Atendía a las flores ya marchitas; animaba a seguir adelante a las que apenas florecían. Aprendía, servía, obedecía.

Invernadero de amor

Nací blanca,
muñequita rubia.
Luciérnagas verdes
susurráronme un canto.
Azucena escogida
entre espinas y cardos.
En una burbuja de amor
crióse mi alma.

El campo abierto

A unos pasos del invernadero residía el mundo natural. Era un lugar prohibido, carente, al parecer, de un plan por Dios establecido. Las semillas caían donde las llevara el viento. Ahí germinaban; también florecían. Las margaritas eran vecinas de las palmeras; los cardos tocaban levemente las campanitas; y las enredaderas, con loco frenesí, trepaban hacia el firmamento desnudo, abrazándose al amor de troncos erguidos. A simple vista, nadie cuidaba del campo, abierto a tanto peligro. Sin embargo, un ritmo casi mágico se oía a la distancia. Un orden tácito habitaba a ras del silencio. Los seres, ajenos al seguimiento de leyes vacías, palpitaban de alegría bajo el mismo Sol de vida. ¿Cómo era posible —se preguntaba la tierna flor— que de esa tierra profana, entre tantos contrarios, llegara a surgir una sola música, a veces más alegre que la que entonaban sus compañeras del invernadero? A través del cristal, la flor escuchaba el hechizo de la voz que corría libre hacia el cielo, y contemplaba, callada, el horizonte lejano del campo abierto —*ad cautelam*, se entiende, como se le había dicho, para evitar el posible contagio con aquel desenfreno mortal.

Pensamientos

Respiro,
y un quejido suave
callado
desnudo
penetra hasta el fondo del alma,
y allí queda,
acurrucado en un nido de nostalgias
durmiendo a la oscuridad
de mis tiernas
y ensangrentadas entrañas,
desiertas sin ti.

Así quisiera estar,
como la palmera abrazada a ese poste
acariciando sin límites sus ojos cerrados
hasta abrirlos
con sus lágrimas en las mías
hechas vida eterna
y suave luz de amor.

Sueños de primavera

La pasión brotó de su centro con toda la fuerza de un torrente de abril, y los sentidos despertaron entonces a la nueva condición de su ser, ya para siempre húmeda canción palpitante. En un principio, sus compañeras la animaban con himnos y promesas, con leyendas de otras flores que habían encontrado la paz en el desierto, en el servicio, en la obediencia. La florecita meditaba entonces, y ahogaba, triste, de su música el sonido. Había surgido de una tierra extraordinaria, y creía —como le repetían— que estaba llamada a transformar el mundo de afuera con los frutos más puros de su vida ejemplar.

Ella aún no lo sabía, pero su alma virgen había dado a luz un hijo, ya eterno: el deseo insaciable había nacido, las ganas salvajes de la entrega, la efusión de una pasión que se desbordaba en humores dulces y en ansias de ternuras infinitas. Oh, florecita, mi querida y más íntima amiga, qué lejos estabas de saber que tanta miel en gestación fermentaría en sudores yermos, en lágrimas que todavía salen veloces de tu cuerpo de niña y que engendran, desde tus entretelas, rebaños de suspiros errantes, ánimas en pena de tantos besos ausentes.

En la raíz de tu estrella

En la raíz de tu centro se encuentran
¡oh, estrella mía!
miles de duendes, encantos y sonrisas;
el dulce palpitar de tu energía,
la cálida caricia de tu brisa.

Luna de mi paisaje nocturno
sol de mi conciencia y mi canto
espejo de clamores que gimen,
de origen inciertos, preñados de llanto.

Quisiera beber
de tu arista primera
cual cáliz dormido
tu verdad sempiterna.

En ti, tierna espina volverme,
a solas, contigo, mi amor,
hasta el fondo;
tan clavadita
en tu cuerpo de hombre,
que hasta el alma
en un grito
atravesarnos
quisiera.

Un paseo por el campo

En vano buscó consuelo la flor dentro del invernadero. Sus ansias de amar no encontraron respuesta del cielo. Entonces, la belleza de su primera juventud miró hacia afuera, y una flor salvaje la invitó a soñar.

Al salir del umbral, sintió el calor de un nuevo rayo de Sol que la fortalecía y, mirando hacia atrás, sonrió, complacida, al ver dibujado el divino colorido de su cuerpo en flor sobre el rocío del cristal que dejaba.

La ternura de un primer beso se cercó de espinas fieras, de una voz áspera, de caricias tan ajena. La florecita quería amarlo tan de veras, sanarle sus heridas, borrar su pena, que se dejó arrastrar con él por tinieblas y quimeras. En una tarde de ilusiones plena, se levantó el telón de un mundo prohibido para ella. Con un baile de amor la florecita soñaba, donde una sola sombra larga se formara. Pero del acto pronto la música cesó: dos almas separadas se acercaban; dos figuras en la noche proyectaban. Culpa de tanta pasión en flor, que la cegaba.

Hay manos que sostienen y levantan, y besos que resucitan al alma que se ha ido lejos. Pero la magia del amor sólo actúa ante otras manos que se abran a la par, y en otras bocas que pronuncien ese ensalmo de miel que llega al alma y recorre el cuerpo en un espasmo de júbilo, de miembros que se lanzan al encuentro de lo que es suyo, y que lo reclaman en un abrazo eterno. Y desde entonces el aliento que se respira es ya del otro, de ese querido habitante de nuestra intimidad más húmeda, donde al son de los dos nacen estrellas que no se fugan y ternuras que se funden en blandas gotitas de cielo.

Un amor para recordar

"... y es tan largo el olvido". Su amor acarició mis dieciocho años con la suavidad de un osito de peluche, todavía sentado en mi almohada. ¡Qué decir de ese cariño! Una sonrisa al aire, un beso, una ilusión que se derrama en el alma con la dulzura de unos ojos de niña que quiere ser mujer, y no puede. Una flor libre, juguetona, disfrutaba con intensidad el momento; su alma, tan ajena al tormento que empezaba a inquietar a su querida Marisita. Jugaron juntos al amor un tiempo —tan breve—, y la estela de su partida enterró caricias que aún agonizan en el lejano abrazo de un recuerdo en flor.

En tu oasis

Del dulce oasis de tu cuerpo
mi alma ansía embriagarse un día.
Respirar mi cuerpo en ardiente beso
tu alma toda,
y exhalar del fruto tierno, mi poesía.

Hundirme en la espesura de tus pinos,
plateados corazones de la mar,
beberme de tu tierra el eucalipto
y en la escarcha de tu aliento, naufragar.

Romper el espejo de esta espera
caer en el centro de tu paz
correr por tu valle sin espinas
cantar en tu estrella mi verdad.

Sin cristal sentir.
Gozar.
Fragancia tuya sola
        y flor no más.

Sombras

El paso de un mirlo nada blanco rasgó la tierna herida de la ausencia, y en una hondonada de cardos y huesos secos quedó su corazón de polen, lastimado y solo, aspirando en la agonía el polvo muerto que levantaba un triste vuelo de mentiras.

Un nuevo rayo de Sol renovó poco a poco el tejido roto del deseo. Un hermoso árbol era, fresca sombra placentera. En el campo de sus ramas la florecita niña labraba y, sin quererlo ella, sus hojas verdes la buscaban. Cada día, la idea de su encanto acariciaba, la lisonja de su lengua la extasiaba; disfraces todos de un amor que se ocultaba, idioma extraño a clara flor que en puros sueños se entregaba. Cinco primaveras de ilusiones plenas, palpitantes de amor, de fiel espera, derramadas en la arena de sus manos, de su cuerpo de hombre, de sus labios suspirantes de otro amor, tan lejos de ella.

Delirio

Agujero de blandos pesares,
mi corazón teñía en sangre tu oblación sombría.

Mariposa de cartílagos celestes
cielo gris
lluvia seca
magia sin.

Desde el abismo, me invitas,
hiedra soñada de diamantes,
a bañarme en el silencio de tu escarcha
a beber a fuego lento tus cenizas.

La tierra gime
el mundo olvida
el agua tiembla,
adolorida,
y tú,
noche mía,
erupcionas tus rubíes desde el blando fondo
de mi tesoro
ensangrentado.

En la luna lúgubre del desencanto
la tierra estéril de tu amor ardía.
Y una tierna voz en flor
rasgaba el hielo del cristal herido
con un nuevo racimo de agonías…

> soy gota de llanto
> soy llanto que trina
> soy nota, soy canto
> soy alma que sangra
> gota a gota
> su vida.

Espejismo

Soy una gotita de rocío cristalizado
que elevaste a la condición de estrella.

Mis manos
temblorosas en la aurora
palpitan
ardientes
por tu noche.

Agonizante
mi cuerpo se viste de espejismo
al compás de una música ajena
          tu danza etérea
                    espuma sin carne
                    sin sangre de fiera.

Oh, rey encantado,
simiente de llanto y arena,
¡por qué me hiciste estrella
si de tu lámpara bella
en dura represa de sal
agujas de plateados caudales
saltaron en látigos siderales
e hicieron de esta querella
pedacitos de cristal!

Suspiros

Sueños
vanas ilusiones
en sudarios blancos
me acompañan esta noche
plañendo al borde de un sepulcro frío.

Entre tinieblas asedian mi imagen
desolada y triste
que se deshoja,
sola,
en el rincón olvidado
de un lejano invernadero.

Mi vida hilvanó con caricias
tu estampa.
Cuántas veces tus manos
cuántas tus labios
entre el paño tibio
que mi ilusión tejiera.

Tristes gotas de dolor
saltaron esta noche de mi alma
bebidas por tentáculos insensibles
secos
pisadas sin piedad
olvidadas
en la verde oscuridad de esta alfombra,
penosa compañía
de un destierro infinito.

Una noche más

Siete años después de nuestro adiós de niños, pasaste por mi vida nuevamente. Recordé entonces nuestro amor en flor, y de tu capullo joven, sus locas ansias, simiente que fecundó mi alma con hijos que aún te buscan, ahogándose, uno a uno, en un doloroso torrente de sangre y de esperanzas heridas entre mis sábanas blancas. Así me encontraste, cariño sólo de cuerpo ausente, con la pasión amordazada de un deseo fiero, vedado de mi paraíso de mujer por sordas voces que, entre letanías y aleluyas, elevaban al Sol su desconcierto, la crudelísima sentencia de una muerte en vida: mi cuerpo en flor, tesoro tan divino, tiritando de amor, tras el impenetrable cristal de un escaparate frío.

Y salimos una noche de la mano. Entre el ruido de la sala comentamos nuestros sueños más queridos. Yo te enseñé mi alma entonces —abierta desde siempre a tu cariño. Te conté de mis ansias doloridas, de mis anhelos de entregarme aún florida, de mi larga espera, por tantos rechazada, profundamente incomprendida. Y tu cuerpo, por esencia diferente cautivado, en la frente con un beso me dejaba; mi fragancia en flor, con alto sacrificio conservada, tú, como otros, despreciabas.

No te culpo ahora por no querer un amor de ilusiones solas hasta que en compromiso nupcial me regalara —día no tan lejano para ti como pensabas. Te culpo sí por cerrar el alma ante la angustia que a la mía desolaba; por no quererme lo suficiente como para atreverte a rescatarme con el peso de tu cuerpo de hombre, purificando con tu entrega el oscuro veneno que hacía años teñía mis venas.

Tu Marisita ya estaba enferma, y sospecha no tenía. De su primer viaje al campo abierto regresó con tal pesar, con tal melancolía, que en el invernadero de nuevo se amparó; propósitos de ser mejor reflorecían. Nuevos guías la cuidaban; mayores penitencias procuraban. Su alma, triste, aceptaba; su cuerpo entero se cerraba; indicios todos del mal que, oculto, la atacaba. Pasarían diez años más hasta que de un diagnóstico se hablara, misteriosa afección que contrajo su cuerpo en flor, aterido por un eterno rocío de plegarias.

Ausencia de ti

Sentirte ausente es lo que más mi alma horada
saberte ido
navegando en otros ojos vivos
cuando los míos mueren en torrentes tristes,
en recuerdos mudos
que no existen.

Gotas de mi ser derramadas
vacíanme de un ayer que no fue mío.

Tus ojos en mi alma
durante largas horas me visitan
y en cada rincón contemplan
imágenes rotas
sueños no soñados
          y mis manos abiertas.

Esperanzas heridas

A la distancia, tu voz, madura ya, intentó excusarse por una ausencia no anunciada. Que me querías demasiado entonces —dijiste— y que por eso me dejabas. Largas horas en mi alma, tus palabras resonaban. Imposible entender tu partida, tan callada. Cuando uno ama de verdad, acerca el alma, comparte penas y esperanzas, escucha el grito de una lágrima; acaricia manos temblorosas, besa con devoción labios cansados, acompaña los pasos de un cuerpo que se amó y que, desde el silencio, se sigue amando.

Tú querías vivir entonces el momento, caro Manolo de mi alma, sin amarres ni pesares, libre de tu niña en flor, que el alma en pena desangraba y el cuerpo claro reservaba. Tres años después te casabas, con un cuerpo en cuya alma no morabas. ¿Que me amabas y por eso me dejabas? El amor verdadero nunca muere —tarde susurró mi alma. Ama a la distancia lo que el cuerpo, enfermo, poder no alcanza. Tu amor pudo sanarme —lo sé bien—, y entonces no me amaste, como ahora no me amas.

Recuerdos

Las niñas de mis ojos con embeleso te contemplan
y mis ansias se escapan, locas, de mi boca.

Oh, recuerdo, que en mi mente vives
y jamás presencia de carne cobras.
Corpus poético te sueño
y en mi lecho sólo idea, quimera
y niebla.

Besándote vivo
en mis noches de recuerdos no nacidos
pero al fin recuerdos hechos
no con la experiencia de una vida
sino con la vida de una idea
que sale presurosa de su celda
recorre paraísos ya prohibidos
y regresa preñada de deseos,
pasiones virginales que
en ardiente frenesí
me despiertan a un mundo delirante
y me ayudan
a no morir viviendo.

Soy una flor que perece de frío.
Escarchas de abandono hielan mis huesos
raíces anegadas de mentiras
y mis pétalos,
pálidos pensamientos,
derramándose desnudos
en cada noche infinita.

Porque tantos ojos que una vez me vieron
dejaron en mí la huella fatídica
de un adiós —no, gracias—
que, al ponerse el Sol,
conforma el mismo oasis de ilusiones
sobre el eco de tu voz adormecida.

Fragancia de mujer

Día y noche transito por calles y veredas, callejones dormidos en el fondo misterioso de una idea. Habitas en mí desde hace tanto, que el solo recuerdo de tu imagen aviva la ilusión de una esperanza casi ciega. Años ha que te busco en el susurro de una voz presa en el tiempo. Cuando despierto al calor del plenilunio de sonrisas con que mi albor se cubre —tantas veces—, un suspiro, desierto de tu estampa, emite el más dulce pensamiento: estar contigo.

Búscote desde mi centro herido, supurando gotas de miel que se pierden lejos de tu boca. ¿Cuándo acariciarás mi tallo y calmarás el ardor de mis hojas, de mis pétalos, de mi polen, cuándo? ¿Cuándo tu capullo, amor, bautizará mis hondas raíces blancas? Flor salvaje es lo que quiero ser ahora, correr libre bajo el Sol por prados sin fronteras, arrancándome de prisa vendas que se asoman a la puerta de este trozo de cristal enterrado hasta el fondo de mi espera y, ya plena de mí, descansar desnuda entre tus brazos, tuya para siempre, embriagante fragancia húmeda de hembra.

Disonancia

Un árbol señero visitó un día el oscuro invernadero. La melodía de su voz atrajo el ardor de su tierna ánima en celo. Reposar bajo su sombra sus plegarias parecía contestar, y juntos ambos empezaron un suave canto a elevar. A varón justo ella quería acompañar; en el monte habríalo hallado con más facilidad. Caminaron poco tiempo por la senda del Señor, y el cielo, abierto de ilusiones, de temores se cubrió. La música, en tono áspero tornó; caricias, en celos fieros descargó; pereza, de repente descubrió; sumisión y obediencia, a la niña le exigió. Mundos ajenos jamás podrán congeniar; de la miel de las flores degustar no puede el salvaje paladar.

Fuga

Vaciaríame de mí esta noche
si posible fuera
y desterraría del alma tanta pena negra.
Sueños, ilusiones, quimeras,
un amor que haber querido quisiera.

Si salir de mí pudiera,
volaría de mi cuerpo a gran distancia;
ya idea y no persona,
ni flor ni dulzura alguna en mí existiera.

Porque en el interior de mi alma
yacen recuerdos heridos
llagas profundas de ensueños rotos
espectros dormidos que asoman silentes
testigos vivos de un dolor que no cesa.

Tu arista, mi pena

Esposo es aquél que reclina la cabeza
sobre el regazo de su fiel amada.
Sollozos, lágrimas, caricias fieras,
plata y marfil, pálido oro,
miel de amor que se funde en un beso
en la húmeda hiedra
hasta el último poro.

Luz que perforas mis entrañas
con la mágica sonrisa de sus ojos puros,
clavaste para siempre en mi alma
el aroma tibio de su ardor en celo.

En la raíz de su estrella soñé un día,
y un llanto de niña se hizo escarcha y arena.

Lamento

Suaves pétalos heridos por la hiel de una ausencia
tiritan, solos, ante un día que no llega.

Mi pequeño santuario desierto
de ojos
de manos
de besos
suspira por un riego eterno de sangre
de raíces largas
de palabras de miel
que mil tequieros derramen
en el pozo olvidado de tantos labios sedientos.

Un polen que duerme oculto en profundidades
eternas madurando ideas
engendra hijos que se alzan al vuelo de mariposas,
duendes que habitan estrellas fugaces
y abandonan,
sin alma,
una débil fragancia de madreselva.

El viento me acaricia
cada noche con su canto de hombre,
y mis tejidos,
atados,
lloran a lo lejos.

Tormenta del desierto

Volaste por mi campo un día después, hierba que parecías buena. Tu cuerpo espigado, la suavidad de tu piel, la dulzura de tus besos me hicieron soñar con un mundo encantado, por caras ninfas habitado. De tu brazo el caminar seguro parecía; tus atenciones, tantas; tu música, tan querida. Los angelitos lavaban la ciudad, y tú te extasiabas —así lo creía— en las mil ocurrencias de una niña. Una tarde de pasión te asomaste al agua clara de mi alma. Una mirada apenas no aguantaste y, asustado, te alejaste; demasiado perfecta para la tuya, sentenciaste. En menos de nueve horas, la menta de tu voz parió infinitas larvas que horadaron mi centro herido, nido ensangrentado que albergaba entonces la jauría de una nueva cría de mentiras.

Calvario

Si el calvario fuera uno
morir no sería una agonía continua.
Moriríase una vez, y punto.
Pero heraldos negros de cerca nos persiguen
y cada día da a luz mañanas de vía crucis infinitos
de noches oscuras
de llantos sin fin.

Y soñamos con el día de la gloria.
Pensamos: ya pasó mi calvario.
Ahora me toca vivir un rato
cosechar sonrisas y claveles
beber miradas y estrenar abrazos.

¡Oh, espejismo, el sueño que desea plenitud de vida!
Los días son amargas gotas que anegan
unos pies que caminan solos
que solos peregrinan en busca de otros
que nunca se encuentran
que se han ido
o que no han llegado todavía.

Estrellas

Son pocos, pero algunos momentos brillarán para siempre en el inmortal firmamento del deseo: una primera mirada, la suave presión de un cuerpo que abraza, la inesperada humedad de un beso que inexplicablemente dice adiós, y la magia de aquella llamada casi a mitad del camino.

Resurrección

Mi alma evoca tu cuerpo en el silencio
al oírte en el tiempo de un espacio ya ausente.

Recordar tu voz ese viernes de otoño
escuchar de tus labios la mención de mi nombre
sentir una ráfaga de suave violencia
en mi espíritu tu voz
tu aliento hecho palabra
mi nombre en tus labios invocando sentimiento
un bautismo de amor
un nuevo sacramento.

Tu palabra me transporta a un tiempo ya ido
donde quedó prisionero mi deseo de amarte
envuelto en un sudario de besos marchitos
de nanas que lloran
calladas
el sueño de una lenta muerte de asfixia.

Un adiós que no quiere decirse
resucita el espectro de un canto ya mudo.
Fuera de mí observo su rostro
su sonrisa de niña
su ternura infinita
su alma que duerme a la espera de un cuerpo
su cuerpo que sufre agonías impías.

Desnudo y herido
mi ser
todo tuyo
solloza de nuevo al decirte otro adiós.

Cariño mío,
tanto amor goces con ella
como tu niña en flor
otra vez
te ofreció.

Azul

Mis caricias recién nacidas
saltaron
desnudas
a un mundo verde
locas por saciar tus ansias
una
a
una
y las mías ahogar en tu paz,
amado capullo de mi alma.

Pero ya son azules mis manos hermosas
y azules gotas destiñen a diario un pálido rostro
que soñó una aurora con sonrisas y esmeraldas
y se desangró de ilusiones soñando,
solo,
a la distancia.

Y es que en tu cuerpo crecieron azules alas
que volaron lejos
y el silencio que dejaste es ya un cielo azul
que empaña el alma.
Tu fondo verde
tus manos largas
tu esencia plena
despreciando mi humedad en flor
hoy como antes

por otro aroma menos dulce
por unos ojos no tan claros
y por un cuerpo, amor,
que jamás podrá bailar
al cálido compás
de la que fuera nuestra alma.

Y esa luz que alumbraba de mi centro
la más recóndita palabra
es ya penumbra triste, azul escarcha.
Mi campo, verde un día,
mi monte, ambrosía en canto,
azules recuerdos de una vida herida,
de todos, el más triste camposanto.

Gracias

Majestuosos árboles, fuertes troncos, diversas especies de la mar se acercaron a admirar de la flor su santidad. Tantos pasaron por su vida, suspirando por su amor, tantos que de ella querían cuerpo, alma y honor. A todos ellos la flor les da las gracias por su camino cruzar, enseñándole lecciones de vida, de amor y de verdad. También les pide perdón por no poderles regalar lo que de ella pretendieron sin engaño y sin maldad.

Una mirada atrás

Hace años ya que la flor medita profundamente. Recuerda tanta pasión perdida, tanta música dormida. Reflexiona hoy sobre su conducta pasada; tantas normas vacías, tantas noches heladas. El alma, es cierto, primero se da; de a poquito —le han dicho—, para más seguridad. Sin su aliento es imposible llegar a lo demás, que es el cuerpo que se entrega en pura danza nupcial. Amor en cuerpo y alma es boda de verdad, una boda de dos almas en dos cuerpos que se dan.

Quisiera la flor ahora en el tiempo regresar, y amar a cuerpo entero con su alma angelical. Misión para ella ya imposible de lograr, como empeñarse tantos en cuerpo y alma separar. Un rayo de Amor fundió ánima y carne en una sola realidad. No besar con el alma es besar con falsedad.

Tocando fondo

Un encuentro no lejano hirió tan hondo su ser, que de su cuerpo el grito la hizo estremecer. Era un árbol marchito —ahora claro lo ve—, un espectro vacío, una fosa de hiel. La flor, tierna todavía, quería su amor aplicar a tantas feas heridas y tantos tormentos curar. Junto a su alma pura, su cuerpo de niña entregar, guardado con tanta dulzura en noches de eterno cristal.

Las náuseas de antes volvieron, con la misma intensidad, producto de aquel veneno que su pasión quiso arrancar. Él intentó ser paciente, ayudarla con suavidad, pero la flor no podía sus tensos pétalos doblar. La paciencia de sus manos se volvió temeridad, y su voz, que la encantaba, miedo puro y ansiedad. Huyó la niña, asustada, de una tierra tan hostil, pisados sus sueños en vida, sus caras ilusiones de abril.

Una mirada por dentro

Presta en busca de respuesta pertinente se marchó. Varios médicos la vieron hasta que un diagnóstico le dieron. Un caso extremo de disfunción interior acusaba; un largo tratamiento la esperaba. Aprendió lo que pudo de esta afección, que de sus orígenes los traumas muchas veces son. La flor analizó cada detalle de su vida, cada encuentro, cada espina, cada fragancia amiga. Observó sus creencias, sus patrones, sus porfías; sus momentos de alegría, sus rechazos, sus heridas.

Pronto recordó un malestar, un temblor que la invadía con cada beso de amor que su cuerpo estremecía. Cuando el beso pasaba a un preludio nupcial, de su interior las náuseas eran ya cosa normal. Bañada en su dulce humedad, un íntimo dolor la comprimía. Con nadie podía hablar la flor de su agonía. Oración y distancia sus guías prescribían; evitar así el pecado que el cuerpo cometía. La niña aguantaba en llantos latigazos que la herían. Músculos preparados para abrirse a la entrega, con una orden de retirada, encogían en súbitas contracciones sus mil venas. Las náuseas se hacían entonces más severas; el dolor, más profundo, en sus selladas entretelas.

Hechizo cruel

En el sigilo del invernadero, un virus mortal crecía a la sombra de una sotana roída por el tiempo. Cuando la semillita, dormida, abrió por primera vez sus ojos puros al cielo, una gasa oscura nubló el fulgor del Sol que penetraba con brío hasta el fondo del cristal frío. Entre las paredes vigilantes, coros de voces sordas repetían desde hacía siglos el mismo canto universal: "La carne había que guardar intacta, inmaculada, incorrupta, indefinidamente; matar sus ansias, una a una, so pena de condenación segura". El impío son surtió en la niña su encanto mortal. El pavor a pecar dominaba ya su mente, su espíritu transparente y, de su carne sensual, cada rincón ardiente.

Herida

Oh, daga,
que cortas
una
a
una
mis transparentes aristas;
tajo profundo
que mi ansia primera segara;
blasfemia de un Sol
que calentarnos odiara.

Ilusiones, besos, caricias,
una fiesta a lo lejos.

Suspiros helados
largas procesiones de plegarias
caminando descalzas
                        por dentro
empañando con sangre de niña
el filo traidor
de un impío cristal enterrado
                        hasta el fondo
de mi alma
de mi cuerpo,
espacio sacrosanto,
                        un oscuro, un eterno sacrilegio
                        en sigilo conformando.

El precio de la virtud

Una flor obediente quería en el cielo morar. Creía que sus guías la iban a cuidar. Que esperara, paciente, a que su amado llegara; que la virtud fortalecía, que de ella un monumento esculpiría, que para otras flores ejemplo serviría. La dulce flor llegó a tal perfección, que tras el cristal del invernadero solita se quedó. Tantos ojos contemplaban su hermosura, tantos deseaban su figura, pero ninguno a tomarla se atrevía; pensarlo era profanación, casi idolatría; en icono de santidad, para su mal, se convertía.

Veinte años de náuseas y escalofríos, diez del recuerdo de la primera contracción de dolor, un alma y un cuerpo heridos por voces sordas, una flor que se deshoja sola, una música que se ahoga por dentro, gotas derramadas al viento, yo.

Atada

No hubo causas físicas, pero en dolorosa disfunción el mal se convirtió. Entró por el espíritu a la mente y, de ahí las órdenes, a cada rincón pertinente. Para el que todavía se muestre no creyente, intente vedar de su cuerpo la pasión correspondiente durante veinte años de contracciones inclementes. Un hondo malestar de espíritu pasará al cuerpo estomacal; náuseas y repugnancias tantas por miedo a actuar mal. Si se encuentra entre los brazos de un amor correspondido, y del espíritu las voces amainan su sordo grito, la mente redoblará esfuerzos para no perder el sitio; invisibles mensajeros enviará, que con lazos y cordeles los músculos refrenen. El cuerpo, sin embargo, seguirá su ritmo sexual; para eso fue hecho por alto designio inmortal. Cuando la restricción se extiende por años sin término y, en vez de dulzuras, los músculos amarres sólo comprenden, llegará el triste día —aquel día de septiembre— cuando ninguna caricia logrará romper ya el coral que aprisiona un oculto fondo angelical.

Desatadlo, y dejadlo andar.

—Juan 11:44

Oscuridad

El proceso de recuperación ha sido lento y complejo; la rehabilitación, intensa; más que infinita la pérdida. Venas dilatadas en manantiales de sangre, músculos y tejidos comprimidos, ya impenetrables, por largos nervios traspasados, sus raíces al aire, ardientes púas perforando mi ser ante el suave contacto deseado por años ya tantos.

Mi dolor en flor reclamaba entonces un potente bálsamo medicinal, y del Sol el calor de Su amor providencial. —No serían, de momento, aquellas manos largas con las que la niña soñaba que una noche la salvaran; sus hermosas manos rubias, en íntima caricia, las que, a su vez, de él las manos rescataran.

Hubo días eternos de agonía y de espanto. Bajo una tormenta perpetua parecía la flor habitar, y de la tormenta el ojo entero sentía sobre ella estallar. El cielo, sereno, a lo lejos, en amable claridad. Cuando vio la flor que la tormenta se forjaba desde su fondo más santo, arrasando cada poro, cada espacio y cada vaso, y que su campo, verde un día, era azul y oscuro llanto, ojo de la tormenta todo, hiriéndola en mortal cuidado, tuvo que recoger solita sus pétalos maltratados, su polen despreciado, su aroma fresco rechazado, y salvar, valiente, su cuerpo y su espíritu, una sola pasión, un solo amor crucificado.

Un baile de primavera

Hoy la flor corre libre por el campo abierto. Su cuerpo claro, por tanto tiempo silenciado, se purifica, desnudo, en el grito que fluye con ansias de su centro herido, torrente que se derrama hasta el fondo de una tierra ensangrentada, de profundas raíces, por siempre blancas, habitada.

Bajo el Sol radiante de abril, la bella niña en flor se viste de verde, y sueña, una vez más, con aquel idílico baile que acaricie la noche que se acerca con el mágico vaivén de una sola sombra larga enamorada.

Respirando el calor sagrado del Sol,
adormecida entre la espesura de tus manos blancas
–eucalipto y plata en rubias eras enredados–,
húmeda fragancia de hembra jugando contigo,
con mis manos de niña, con tu cuerpo de hombre,
a un tú y yo, por siempre amor.

El que tenga oídos para oír,

que oiga.

—Lucas 8:8

Glosario

CRNP. *Certified Registered Nurse Practitioner.* Enfermero(a) especialista titulado(a). En Estados Unidos, enfermero(a) especializado(a) tanto en el diagnóstico físico y psicosocial de los pacientes, como en su tratamiento. Por su capacitación, puede recetar medicamentos y llevar a cabo varios procedimientos médicos.

disfunción sexual. Trastorno del funcionamiento normal de la sexualidad al alterarse cuantitativa o cualitativamente alguno de sus componentes: la mente (pensamientos y emociones) o el cuerpo (sistema nervioso, circulatorio, muscular y endocrino). Los factores físicos suelen conducir a problemas psicológicos, y los psicológicos, a su vez, crean o agravan problemas físicos.

dispareunia. Coito doloroso o intento de coito doloroso. Dolor profundo genital o pélvico que experimenta la mujer antes, durante o después del coito. Puede originarse por un trauma local (entre otros: malformación congénita, infección, inflamación de las glándulas vestibulares, deficiencia estrogénica, tumores) o por factores psicológicos (vaginismo).

EdD. *Educationis Doctor*. Doctor(a) en Educación.

fondo pélvico. También llamado **suelo pélvico** o **piso pélvico.** Músculos, ligamentos y tejidos que se encuentran en la base del abdomen, cuya estructura en forma de hamaca sostiene el útero, la vejiga, la uretra y el recto. Los músculos del fondo pélvico se conocen también como "músculos del amor" puesto que en la mujer juegan un papel de primerísima importancia. Se utilizan durante las relaciones sexuales, el embarazo y el parto, así como en la evacuación de la orina y de las heces. Reaccionan a la tos, a la risa, al estornudo y a las contracciones del abdomen. Cuando estos músculos se debilitan, parte de la fisioterapia consiste en los ejercicios de Kegel (*Kegel exercises*), así llamados por Arnold H. Kegel, ginecólogo y obstetra estadounidense del s. XX.

herejía. (en sentido figurado) Gran daño o tormento inflingido injustamente contra una persona.

LPC. *Licensed Professional Counselor.* Consejero(a) titulado(a) y autorizado(a) para ejercer.

MA. *Magister Artium* (m.), *Magistra Artium* (f.). Máster en Artes.

MD. *Medicinae Doctor.* Doctor(a) en Medicina.

MPT. *Master of Physical Therapy.* Máster en fisioterapia.

NCC. *National Certified Counselor.* Consejero(a) titulado(a) y autorizado(a) para ejercer a nivel nacional.

PhD. *Philosophiae Doctor.* Doctor(a) en Filosofía y Letras.

psicógeno. (adjetivo) Que se origina en la mente o en un conflicto mental o emocional.

vaginismo. Contracción involuntaria condicionada repentina y dolorosa de los músculos vaginales inferiores. Se origina por el deseo consciente o inconsciente de la mujer a evitar la penetración. Entre los factores físicos responsables por su padecimiento destacan las lesiones, las úlceras y la inflamación de la vagina. Entre los psicológicos, los más frecuentes son los traumas sexuales: violación, incesto, miedo o aversión al coito, una atmósfera represiva familiar y la práctica religiosa centrada en el control de un cuerpo que se percibe como enemigo del espíritu y obstáculo para la salvación eterna.

vestibulitis vulvar. Inflamación del vestíbulo vulvar. Es uno de varios síndromes de dolor vulvar que conllevan a la dispareunia. Véase **vulvodinia**.

vulvodinia. Literalmente, "vulva dolorosa". El término se refiere a varios trastornos dolorosos que afectan a los órganos genitales femeninos. Entre los más comunes, destaca el síndrome de vestibulitis vulvar (*vulvar vestibulitis syndrome, VVS*), caracterizado por la inflamación de las glándulas vestibulares: glándulas de Bartholin (por el anatomista danés Caspar Bartholin Secundus, 1655-1738) y glándulas de Skene (por el famoso ginecólogo escocés que emigrara a los EE.UU., Alexander Johnson Chalmers Skene, 1837-1900). Aunque la causa no se ha determinado todavía, varios factores pueden contribuir a su aparición: infecciones, irritaciones y lesiones neuromusculares. Como resultado, el vestíbulo se inflama y las glándulas se hipersensibilizan (permaneciendo ambos así a menos que se procure atención médica), lo que hace que cualquier contacto —bien neutral (tampones), bien estimulante (penetración sexual)— produzca dolor físico y ardor intolerables. Para más detalles, véase el panfleto informativo de Susan Kellogg-Spadt, PhD, Managing Vulvar Vestibulitis and Sexual Pain: A Guide for Women and Their Partners (Cómo controlar la vestibulitis vulvar y el dolor sexual: una guía para la mujer y su pareja), 2001; y el artículo "Vulvar Vestibulitis and Sexual Pain: New Insights" ("Vestibulitis vulvar y dolor sexual:

nuevas perspectivas"), publicado por Susan Kellogg-Spadt, PhD, y Jennifer L. Giordano, EdD, en la revista The Female Patient, Vol. 27, abril, 2002.

De la presente edición:
Housed Under Glass / Tras paredes de cristal
por María Luisa Ortega Hernández,
producida por la casa editorial CBH Books
(Lawrence, Massachusetts, Estados Unidos)
e impresa en los talleres poligráficos de Quebec,
Canadá Año 2006.
Cualquier comentario sobre esta obra
o solicitud de permisos, puede escribir a:
Departamento de español
Cambridge BrickHouse, Inc.
60 Island Street Lawrence,
MA 01840, U.S.A.
o directamente a la autora:
ortegaml_dr@yahoo.com